ARE FUN TO MAKE, SEE HISS AND HERSS ON 28

All about Wool

Knitting is a way of joining threads to make fabric. This is done by using the thread to form many loops.

Knitting is a very old craft. No one knows for certain when people started knitting, but pieces of knitted fabric have been found that are 3000 years old.

In nomadic Arab tribes the women would spin while their husbands would knit, and in the Middle Ages knitting was mostly done by men in special groups called guilds. In these guilds men would serve a six year apprenticeship before becoming Master Knitters.

Today knitting is not only performed by individuals, but also by large knitting machines in factories. Knitting is a very useful skill and can be used to make a wide range of things.

What is wool?

Wool is a fibre. A fibre is a thin, thread-like substance.

Some fibres come from animals and some from plants. These are called natural fibres. Wool is a natural fibre. It comes from sheep. Mohair comes from goats. Cotton comes from the cotton plant and linen comes from the flax plant.

Some fibres are human-made. They are invented by scientists and made in factories. They are called synthetic fibres. Nylon and acrylic are two synthetic fibres.

Wool grows out of the sheep's skin in the same way that a cat's fur does.

Wool in Australia

Some countries produce a lot of wool. It is sold to other countries and makes them a lot of money.

Sheep taken from England to Australia by early settlers on sailing ships were for food and wool.

Because the Australian climate was suitable for grazing sheep, the numbers grew until today there are about 166 million sheep. This has made Australia one of the largest producers of wool in the world. The very best wool comes from the famous Merino sheep which has a thick but fine fleece.

What is wool like?

Wool is different from fur or hair in ways that make it a very special and useful fibre. It is also unlike plant fibres and synthetics.

Wool is not straight. It grows in very fine waves. These waves are called crimps.

LET'S GET RAPT IN WOOL

The crimps make wool very springy and elastic. This means that when it is made into jumpers and cardigans they return to their original shape after being worn and stretched, and they do not become creased and crumpled.

Each fibre of wool has many scales. These scales make the wool fibres stick together easily. They also help stop the wool becoming too wet. Wool absorbs moisture and can become quite wet with -out feeling damp or cold. This means if you are caught in the rain you are less likely to get a chill wearing woollen clothes. So wool is always the best thing to wear in cold or damp weather.

Wool can absorb perspiration. It also allows air to circulate near your body and does not cling to you.

Because it absorbs moisture, wool dyes well. Wool is a good insulator. This means that it keeps the cold out in winter, and the heat out in summer. No human-made fibre has this quality.

A sheep with a thick coat of wool in summer is not as hot as it looks. Lightweight woollen clothes can actually keep you cool in summer.

Wool is coated with a protective covering of wool grease called lanoline. Lanoline helps to make the wool waterproof. Usually the lanoline is washed out of the wool before spinning, but sometimes it is left in for garments like ski jumpers which need to be extra waterproof.

Because it is waterproof, wool does not absorb stains quickly. So if you spill something on it, you can wipe it off quite easily.

Wool is a very light and strong fibre. It resists wear and tear and lasts for years.

A most important quality of wool is that it is flame resistant. It does not burn easily. So it is a very safe fibre.

Firemen wear wool suits and so do racing drivers. Anyone working where fire is a danger should wear wool.

If there are open heaters or fires in your home you should never wear synthetic or cotton pyjamas or dressing gowns. Woollen ones are much safer. Human-made fibres and cotton burn quickly, and people can burn to death if their clothes catch fire.

A wool blanket is a good way to put out a fire. You must throw it over the flames to smother them.

How is wool processed?

First the wool must be taken from the sheep by shearing it off with electric clippers. This does not hurt the sheep — it is just like having your hair cut.

After the wool is shorn from the sheep it is called a fleece. The fleeces are trimmed of dirty and ragged edges, sorted and packed into big bales to be sold at wool auctions. The buyers then take it to the factories.

At the factory the wool is first washed. Then it is combed to remove the burrs, seeds, tangles and dirt. Next it is dyed in different colours, and then it is spun into long threads and wound on spools. Then it is ready to be woven or knitted into lengths of fabric on big machines.

How to identify wool

The Woolmark

PURE NEW WOOL

Some human-made fibres look rather like wool. The only way to be sure you are buying real wool is to look on the label for the Woolmark. The Woolmark is used all over the world to tell people they are buying pure new wool.

How to Knit

CASTING ON

Before you start to knit, you have to put some stitches on the needles. This is called *casting on*. (You might find casting on a little tricky — see the note to parents below — but when you're ready here's how you do it.)

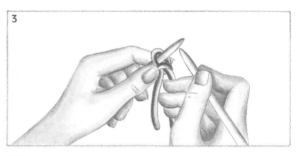

3 Hold the other needle as you would hold a pencil.

1 Tie the end of the yarn around one of your needles.

2 Pull the loop through so the knot rests under the needle. Put this needle into your left hand.

4 Push the point of the right-hand needle through the front part of the loop on the left-hand needle.

Note to parents:
Children often find the hardest part of learning to knit is casting on. To prevent their enthusiasm waning, it may be a good idea to cast on for them, and leave learning to cast on until they have started to develop their knitting skills.

5 Holding the yarn in your right hand, put it around the top of the right-hand needle.

6 Draw the yarn through the loop on the left-hand needle, so making a new loop.

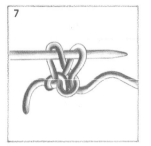

7 Slip the new loop onto the left-hand needle. You now have two stitches.

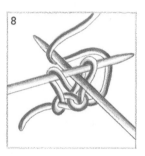

8 Now put the point of your right-hand needle behind the new stitch and put the yarn around the top of the right-hand needle.

9 Draw the yarn through the loop on the left-hand needle.

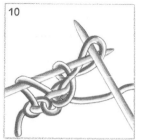

10 Put the new loop on the left-hand needle. You now have three stitches.

Continue in this way until you have as many stitches as you want.

PLAIN OR GARTER STITCH

If you knit every row using plain or garter stitch (also known as knit stitch), you will knit a pattern called garter stitch.

11 Hold the needle with your cast-on stitches in

12 Holding the yarn in your right hand, put it around the top of the right-hand needle.

13 Pull the loop through the stitch using your right-hand needle.

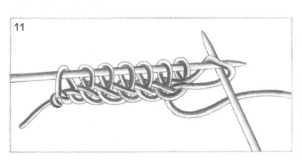

your left hand. Push the point of your right-hand needle through the middle of the first stitch.

8

14 Making sure the new loop stays on your right-hand needle, gently slip the first stitch off your left-hand needle.

15 Push the point of your right-hand needle through the middle of the next stitch. Put the yarn around the top of the right-hand needle, and pull the loop through the stitch using your right-hand needle.

16 Making sure the new loop stays on your right-hand needle, gently slip the first stitch off your left-hand needle. You now have two stitches on your right-hand needle.

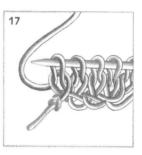

17 Follow the same steps with every stitch and you will have knitted a row. Now all your stitches are on the right-hand needle.

18 Put the needle with the stitches on it in your

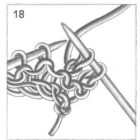

left hand and the empty needle in your right hand and you are ready to start the second row. Follow the same steps to knit the second row and as many rows as you want.

PURL STITCH

If you knit one row plain and one row purl you will knit a pattern called stocking stitch. The smooth side is called the 'knit' side and the rough side (the one with the ridges) is called the 'purl' side.

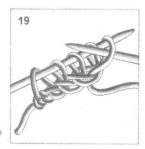

19 Hold the needle with the cast-on stitches in your left hand. Put the right-hand needle into the front of the first stitch and in front of the left-hand needle.

20 Holding the yarn in your right hand, bring it to the front of the right-hand needle, then put it around the tip of that needle.

21 Draw the loop through the stitch keeping it on the right-hand needle which is now behind the left-hand needle.

22 Gently slip the first stitch off the left-hand needle.

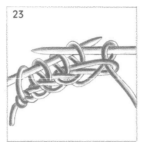

23 Put the right-hand needle into the front of the first stitch on the left-hand needle and in front of the left-hand needle. Repeat steps 20 to 22. You will now have two stitches on your left-hand needle.

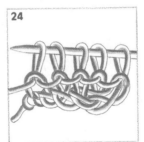

24 Follow the same steps with every stitch and you will have knitted a row. Now all your stitches are on the right-hand needle.

Put the needle with the stitches on it in your left hand and the empty needle in your right-hand and you are ready to start the second row. Follow the same steps to knit the second row and as many rows as you want.

CASTING OFF

Knitting is finished by casting off. Try to cast off as loosely as possible.

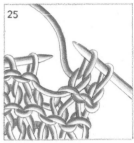

25 Knit two stitches.

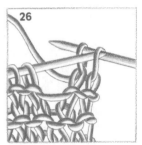

26 Push the point of your left-hand needle into the centre of the first stitch.

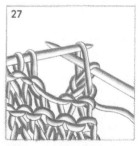

27 Lift the first stitch on your right-hand needle over the second stitch and over the top of the right-hand needle.

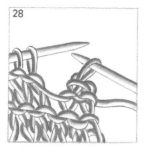

28 Drop the stitch off the needle so that only one stitch remains on the right-hand needle.

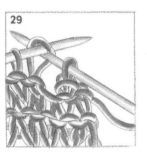

29 Knit another stitch.

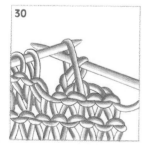

30 Lift the first stitch on your right-hand needle over the second stitch and drop it off the needle as before.

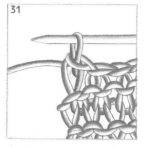

31 Continue on in this way until you have only one stitch left.

32 Break off the yarn, slip the stitch off the needle, put the end of the yarn through the stitch and pull firmly.

CHANGING THE SHAPE OF YOUR KNITTING

The things that you knit do not have to have straight sides. You can change the shape of your knitting by making new stitches (increasing) or getting rid of stitches (decreasing). Adding stitches makes your knitting wider, taking stitches away makes it narrower.

Increasing

33 Push the point of your right-hand needle through the middle of the first stitch, put the yarn around the top of the right-hand needle, and pull the loop through the stitch on the left-hand needle as usual, but don't drop the stitch off the left-hand needle.

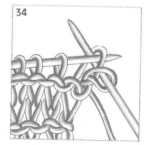

34 Now put the right-hand needle into the first stitch again, but this time through the back of the stitch.

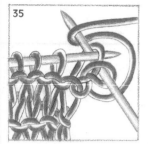

35 Put the wool around the needle and pull the loop through.

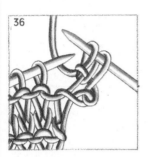

36 Gently slip the stitch off the left-hand needle. You now have two stitches on your right-hand needle, so you have made an extra one.

You can increase at the end of a row too. If you are told to 'increase at the end of a row' repeat steps 33 to 36 on the second last stitch.

Decreasing

You can decrease at the beginning or end of a row by knitting two stitches together. (The illustrations here show the stitches being knitted together at the end of a row.)

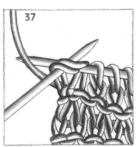

37 Put your right-hand needle through two stitches on the left-hand needle (from left to right for knit stitches and from right to left for purl stitches), put your wool around the right-hand needle, and pull the loop through the two stitches.

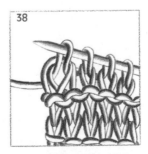

38 Gently slip both stitches off the left-hand needle. You now have one less stitch.

PICKING UP STITCHES

Even the best knitters drop a stitch occasionally. The easiest way to pick up dropped stitches is with a crochet hook. If you are knitting stocking stitch, work with the knit side (the smooth side) facing you. If you are knitting garter stitch, you will need to turn the knitting around each time you pick up a stitch.

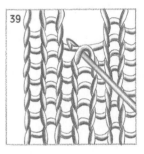

39 Put the hook through the dropped stitch. Catch the straight thread above the dropped stitch and pull this through the dropped stitch. Repeat this step for each of the rows that the stitch has dropped. When the dropped stitch is back in place, slip it onto the needle and continue knitting.

CHANGING COLOUR OR STARTING A NEW BALL

What do you do when your wool runs out or when you want to use a different colour?

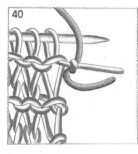

40

40 At the beginning of a row, break off your wool about 10 centimetres from the needle. Tie your new wool onto the strand of old wool with a knot and move the knot along the wool until it is as close as possible to the needle. Then continue knitting in your new colour.

TO KNIT

HAVE A BALL LEARNING

TEAM UP THIS WINTER IN WARM WOOLLEN BRIGHTS

Wrapped Up

Measurements

Length (approx): 80 cm
Width (approx): 14 cm

You will need

8 ply yarn, 50 g balls
Scarf 1 (one colour): 2½ balls
Scarf 2 (even stripes): 1¼ balls 1st Colour, 1¼ balls 2nd Colour
Scarf 3 (striped ends): 1½ balls 1st Colour, 1 ball 2nd Colour, ¼ ball 3rd Colour

1 pair 4.00 mm (No 8) knitting needles, a crochet hook, a piece of cardboard 10 cm x (approx) 15 cm

There's nothing like a warm, woolly scarf to rug up against cold, windy days. And if you are just learning to knit, these scarves are very easy to do.

Scarf 1 ONE COLOUR

Using 4.00 mm needles, cast on 31 stitches.

Knit in garter stitch (every row a knit row) until scarf measures 80 cm. Cast off and darn in ends.

Note: *Ends are darned in so the knitting looks neat and does not unravel. To darn in an end, thread the end of the yarn through a needle then pass the needle in and out of the knitting a few times either along the cast-off edge or along the side. Remove the needle and cut off any part of the end not darned in.*

Following the instructions on page 18, make a fringe on each end of the scarf.

Scarf 2 EVEN STRIPES

Using 4.00 mm needles and 1st Colour, cast on 31 stitches. Knit 14 rows garter stitch. (This means 7 ridges on each side of your scarf.)

Break off yarn. Always leave enough yarn to darn in the end.
Using 2nd Colour, knit 14 rows garter stitch.
Break off yarn.
Repeat last 28 rows until scarf measures about 80 cm finishing with 14 rows in 1st Colour.

Cast off and darn in ends.
Using 1st Colour and following the instructions on page 18, make a fringe on each end of the scarf.

BEAT THE BIG CHILL

Scarf 3 STRIPED ENDS

Using 4.00 mm needles and 1st Colour, cast on 31 stitches.
Knit 8 rows garter stitch. (This means 4 ridges on each side of your scarf.)
Break off yarn. Always leave enough yarn to darn in the end.
Using 2nd Colour, knit 8 rows garter stitch.
Break off yarn.
Using 1st Colour, knit 8 rows garter stitch.
Break off yarn.
Using 2nd Colour, knit 40 rows garter stitch.
Break off yarn.
Using 3rd Colour, knit 8 rows garter stitch.
Break off yarn.
Using 1st Colour, knit in garter stitch until scarf measures 63 cm, finishing at side where all the ends of yarn are.
Break off yarn.
Using 3rd Colour, knit 8 rows garter stitch.
Break off yarn.
Using 2nd Colour, knit 40 rows garter stitch.
Break off yarn.
Using 1st Colour, knit 8 rows garter stitch.
Break off yarn.
Using 2nd Colour, knit 8 rows garter stitch.
Break off yarn.
Using 1st Colour, knit 8 rows garter stitch.
Cast off and darn in ends.
Using 1st Colour and following the adjacent instructions, make a fringe on each end of the scarf.

HOW TO MAKE A FRINGE

Wind yarn around a piece of cardboard 10 cm wide and cut the yarn along one edge. With the wrong side of your knitting facing you, and using a crochet hook, and 2 or more strands of yarn (the diagram shows 4 strands), fold the yarn in half and draw a loop through a stitch on the scarf (diagram 1). Draw the ends of the yarn through this loop (diagram 2), and pull them lightly to form a knot. Diagram 3 shows the right side of the knot.

1

2

3

Topped Off

Keep your brains warm with this woolly cap which looks great teamed with the scarf and mittens.

Measurements
Fits head (approx): 54 cm

You will need
8 ply yarn, 50 g balls
Cap 1 (one colour): 2 balls
Cap 2 (striped): 1¼ balls 1st Colour,
¾ ball 2nd Colour

1 pair 4.00 mm (No 8) knitting needles, a large tapestry needle for finishing off and sewing seams, cardboard and scissors to make a pompom

Cap 1 ONE COLOUR
Using 4.00 mm needles, cast on 110 stitches.
Knit in garter stitch until cap measures 16 cm.

DECREASE FOR TOP OF CAP
1st row K2 (this means to knit 2 stitches), * K2 together (see page 12), K4. Repeat the section beginning from * until the end of the row. You should have 92 stitches left on your needle.
Knit 3 rows garter stitch.
5th row K2, * K2 together, K3. Repeat the section beginning from * until the end of the row. You should have 74 stitches left.
Knit 3 rows garter stitch.
9th row K2, * K2 together, K2. Repeat the section beginning from * until the end of the row. You should have 56 stitches left.
Knit 3 rows garter stitch.
13th row K2, * K2 together, K1. Repeat the section beginning from * until the end of the row. You should have 38 stitches left.
Knit 1 row garter stitch.

15th row K2 together across the whole row. You should have 19 stitches left.

Break off yarn, leaving an end about 30 cm long.

Thread a large tapestry needle with the long end and thread this through the stitches remaining on the needle, slipping the stitches off the needle as you go. Pull up the end tightly (so the top of the cap is gathered) and fasten securely with small stitches, then continue with a flat seam and sew up cap.

Using cardboard 7 cm in diameter with a 1.5 cm centre hole and following the adjacent instructions make a pompom and sew securely to the top of the cap.

HOW TO MAKE A POMPOM

Cut out two circles of cardboard 7 cm in diameter. Cut a round hole in the centre of both circles 1.5 cm in diameter. Put the two circles together and wind the yarn round and round the cardboard until the centre hole is completely filled up. Place the point of a pair of scissors between the two circles of cardboard and cut around the yarn, keeping the scissors between the cardboard circles all the time. Using a double strand of yarn, wrap it round between the two circles of cardboard, knot firmly and take away the cardboard. Trim the pompom.

HOW TO MAKE A POMPOM

Cap 2 STRIPED

Using 4.00 mm needles and 1st Colour, cast on 110 stitches.

Knit 20 rows garter stitch (this means 10 ridges on each side of your work).

Do not break off 1st Colour but join in 2nd Colour.

Knit 2 rows garter stitch.

Before knitting the next row, wind the 2nd Colour once around the 1st Colour so that the 1st Colour can be carried neatly at the side of your work.

Knit 2 rows garter stitch (there should be 2 ridges of 2nd Colour on the right side of your work.)

Do not break off 2nd Colour but pick up 1st Colour again. (Take care not to pull it too tightly or the side of your work will gather up.)

Knit 4 rows garter stitch, winding colours as before after first 2 rows.

Knit in stripes of 4 rows of each colour until cap measures 16 cm, ending with a complete stripe.

Continue to work in 4-row stripes and decrease for top as for Cap 1.

Complete and make up as for Cap 1 using 1st Colour for the pompom.

Finger Rap

Measurements
Fits hand (approx): 15 cm

You will need
8 ply yarn, 50 g balls
Mittens 1 (one colour): 1½ balls
Mittens 2 (striped): 1¼ balls 1st Colour, ¼ ball 2nd Colour
Mittens 3 (contrasting cuff): ½ ball 1st Colour, 1¼ balls 2nd Colour

1 pair 4.00 mm (No 8) knitting needles, a large tapestry needle for finishing off and sewing seams

Mittens 1 ONE COLOUR
Make 2.

Using 4.00 mm needles, cast on 33 stitches. Knit 32 rows in garter stitch. (This means 16 ridges on each side of your work.)

INCREASE FOR HAND
Next row K5 (this means knit 5 stitches), * increase in next stitch (see page 11), K1.

Repeat the section beginning from * until you have 4 stitches left, K4. You should have 45 stitches left on your needle.

Knit 27 rows garter stitch (30 ridges on each side of your work altogether).

** DIVIDE FOR THUMB AND HAND
Next row K16, turn work around and work on these 16 stitches for hand.

Knit in garter stitch until hand measures 9 cm from where you divided for the hand, or the length that suits your hand.

Your final item of armoury in the fight against winter cold, these mittens will keep the tenderest digits safe from frostbite.

SHAPE TOP OF HAND

Next row K2, K2 together (see page 12), K8, K2 together, K2. You should have 14 stitches left on your needle. Knit 1 row garter stitch.
Next row K2, K2 together, K6, K2 together, K2. You should have 12 stitches left on your needle.
Knit 1 row garter stitch.
Cast off.
Join yarn to remaining stitches.

WORK THUMB

Next row K13, turn and work on these 13 stitches for thumb.
Knit in garter stitch until the thumb measures 4 cm from where you divided, or the length that suits your thumb.

SHAPE TOP OF THUMB

Next row K1, * K2 together, K1. Repeat the section from * until end of row.
Break off yarn, leaving an end about 25 cm long.
Thread a large tapestry needle with this long end and thread through the stitches remaining on the needle, slipping the stitches off the needle as you go. Pull up tightly (so the top of the thumb is gathered) and fasten securely with small stitches, then continue with a flat seam and sew seam at side of thumb. Join yarn to remaining 16 stitches.

WORK OTHER SIDE OF HAND

Knit in garter stitch until hand measures 9 cm from where you divided, or the length that suits your hand.

SHAPE TOP OF HAND

Next row K2, K2 together, K8, K2 together, K2. You should have 14 stitches left.
Knit 1 row garter stitch.
Next row K2, K2 together, K6, K2 together, K2. You should have 12 stitches left.
Knit 1 row garter stitch.
Cast off.

MAKE UP

Using a flat seam, sew around the hand of the mitten.

Mittens 2 STRIPED

Make 2.

Using 4.00 mm needles and 1st Colour, cast on 33 stitches.

Knit 32 rows garter stitch. (This means 16 ridges on each side of your work.)

INCREASE FOR HAND

Next row K5 (this means to knit 5 stitches), * increase in next stitch (see page 11), K1. Repeat the section beginning from * until you have 4 stitches left, K4. You should now have 45 stitches.

Knit 1 row garter stitch.

Break off yarn. Always leave enough yarn to darn in end.

Using 2nd Colour, knit 8 rows garter stitch (21 ridges on each side of your work altogether).

Break off yarn.

Using 1st Colour, knit 8 rows garter stitch (25 ridges on each side of your work).

Break off yarn.

Using 2nd Colour, knit 8 rows garter stitch (29 ridges on each side of your work).

Break off yarn.

Using 1st Colour, knit 2 rows garter stitch (30 ridges on each side of your work).

DIVIDE FOR THUMB AND HAND

Next row K16, turn work around and work on these 16 stitches for hand. Knit in garter stitch until hand measures 9 cm from where you divided for the hand, or the length that suits your hand.

SHAPE TOP OF HAND
Next row K2, K2 together, K8, K2 together, K2. You should have 14 stitches left on your needle.
Knit 1 row garter stitch.
Next row K2, K2 together, K6, K2 together, K2. You should have 12 stitches left on your needle.
Knit 1 row garter stitch.
Cast off.
Join yarn to remaining stitches.

WORK THUMB
Next row K13, turn and work on these 13 stitches for thumb.
Knit in garter stitch until thumb measures 4 cm from where you divided for the thumb, or the length that suits your thumb.

SHAPE TOP OF THUMB
Next row K1, * K2 together, K1. Repeat the section from * until end of row.
Break off yarn, leaving an end about 25 cm long.
Thread a large tapestry needle with this long end and thread through the stitches remaining on the needle, slipping the stitches off the needle as you go. Pull up tightly (so the top of the thumb is gathered) and fasten securely with small stitches, then continue with a flat seam and sew seam at side of thumb.
Join yarn to remaining 16 stitches.

WORK OTHER SIDE OF HAND
Knit in garter stitch until hand measures 9 cm from where you divided

for the hand, or the length that suits your hand.

SHAPE TOP OF HAND
Next row K2, K2 together, K8, K2 together, K2. You should have 14 stitches left.
Knit 1 row garter stitch.
Next row K2, K2 together, K6, K2 together, K2. You should have 12 stitches left.
Knit 1 row garter stitch.
Cast off.

MAKE UP
Using a flat seam, sew around the hand of the mitten.

Mittens 3 CONTRASTING CUFF
Make 2.
Using 4.00 mm needles and 1st Colour, cast on 33 stitches.
Knit 32 rows in garter stitch. (This means 16 ridges on each side of your work.)

INCREASE FOR HAND
Next row K5 (this means knit 5 stitches), * increase in next stitch (see page 11), K1. Repeat the section beginning with * until you have 4 stitches left, K4. You should now have 45 stitches.
Knit one row garter stitch.
Break off yarn. Always leave enough yarn to darn in the end.
Using 2nd Colour, knit 26 rows garter stitch. (This means 30 ridges on each side of your work altogether.)
Complete as for Mittens 1 from ** to end.

25

WHAT A GIGGLE, A RAINBOW SERPENT OF

YOUR OWN TO WRIGGLE

Hiss and Herss

You can have lots of fun choosing the colours for your very own rainbow serpent. The squiggly bits on top of the snake are done with French knitting.

Measurements
Length (approx): 150 cm

You will need
8 ply yarn, 50 g balls

2 balls Main Colour (MC), 1 ball 1st Contrast (C1), 1 ball 2nd Contrast (C2), 1 ball 3rd Contrast (C3), small quantity 4th Contrast (C4)

1 pair 4.00 mm (No 8) knitting needles, a knitting nancy (or a hollow cylinder, matches and sticky tape if you want to make your own), a large tapestry needle for sewing seams, polyester or nylon stuffing

Snake
Start at the tail end.

Using 4.00 mm needles and MC, cast on 4 stitches.

1st row Knit, increasing one stitch at beginning and end of row (see page 11).

2nd row Purl.

Repeat 1st and 2nd rows until there are 28 stitches on your needle.

24th row Purl.

25th row Knit.

26th row Purl.

** Using C2, repeat 25th and 26th rows 18 times.

Using C1, repeat 25th and 26th rows 18 times.

Using MC, repeat 25th and 26th rows 18 times.

Using C3, repeat 25th and 26th rows 18 times. **

28

Repeat from ** to ** until work measures approximately 130 cm from beginning, ending with C1.

SHAPE HEAD

Using MC, continue in stocking stitch (1 row knit, 1 row purl) until work measures 142 cm from beginning, ending with a purl row.

Next row Knit, decreasing one stitch at beginning and end of row (see page 12).

Next row Purl.

Repeat last 2 rows until 10 stitches remain on your needle.

Next row Purl.

Cast off.

UNDER HEAD

Using 4.00 mm needles and MC, cast on 10 stitches.

1st row Knit, increasing one stitch at beginning and end of row.

2nd row Purl.

Repeat 1st and 2nd rows until there are 28 stitches on your needle.

24th row Purl.

25th row Knit.

26th row Purl.

27th row Knit, decreasing one stitch at beginning and end of row.

Repeat rows 24 to 27 inclusive until you have 10 stitches left on your needle.

Next row Purl.

Cast off.

SNAKES ALIVE

SQUIGGLES

Using a knitting nancy and MC, make a 25-cm length of French knitting (see next page).
Fasten off.
Make three more 25-cm lengths of knitting using C1, C2 and C3.

MAKE UP

With wrong sides together, and using matching colours, stitch the 2 long edges together, starting at the tail. If you join 2 segments at a time, and then stuff these before sewing up the next segment, you will find it easier to get the snake's body an even thickness. Make sure the tail is well pointed and stuff it firmly.

When you come to the head, join in the under head, sewing all round. Sew the straight edge of the under head piece to the straight edge of the last segment.

Using C4, embroider two eyes on the snake's head in satin stitch as shown. Attach a strand of yarn to the snake's mouth for a tongue. Stitch squiggles randomly to snake's body.

SATIN STITCH FOR
SNAKE'S EYES

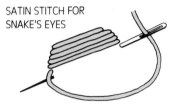

HOW TO MAKE A KNITTING NANCY AND FRENCH KNITTING

To make a knitting nancy, you will need any hollow cylinder (the wider the cylinder, the thicker your cord of knitting), matches (or icy pole sticks for a large cylinder) and sticky tape. Tape the matches around the outside of your cylinder. Make sure they are evenly spaced.

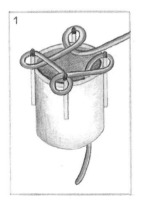

1 Start your French knitting by dropping one end of your yarn through the cylinder so you can

hold it underneath, then wrap it around each of the matches, making sure you wrap all matches in the same direction.

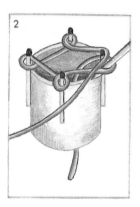

2 Bring your yarn along the outside of the first match. Using a knitting needle or your fingers, lift the bottom loop over this thread and drop it into the centre of the nancy.

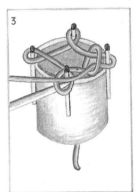

3 Wrap the yarn around the back of the next

match, then lift the bottom loop over the top and drop it into the centre of the nancy. Repeat this for all matches.

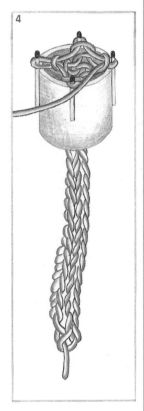

4 Continue in this way and gradually a cord will grow out of the bottom of your nancy. When the cord is long enough, finish off by lifting the loop off each match and threading the end of your yarn through each loop. Pull tight and knot.

Best Dressed Bear

Little sisters and brothers love to dress up their teddy bears, or perhaps you have a little furry friend yourself who would look terrific in this great outfit.

Measurements

To fit teddy bear	Small	Large
Height (from head to toe):		
	30 cm	40 cm
Chest:	34	44

Note: If your teddy bear is small, follow the numbers **outside** the brackets in the pattern. If your teddy bear is large, follow the numbers **inside** the brackets.

You will need

8 ply yarn, 50 g balls

Coat: 1 (2) balls

Socks: 1 (2) balls

Headband: 1 (1) ball

1 pair 4.00 mm (No 8) knitting needles, a large tapestry needle for sewing seams, a 4.00 mm crochet hook and button for the coat

Coat

BACK

Using 4.00 mm needles, cast on 37 (49) stitches.

1st row Knit.

Work in garter stitch (knit every row), until your knitting measures 11 (15) cm from the cast-on row.

Cast off all 37 (49) stitches, leaving a 5 cm length of yarn at end to sew into seam when finishing coat to secure knitting.

FRONTS

Make 2.

Using 4.00 mm needles, cast on 19 (25) stitches.

Work in garter stitch (knit every row), until your knitting measures 11 (15) cm from cast-on row.

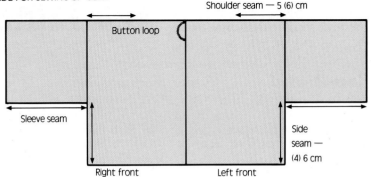

Shoulder seam — 5 (6) cm

Button loop

Sleeve seam

Side seam — (4) 6 cm

Right front   Left front

Cast off all 19 (25) stitches, leaving a 15 cm length of yarn at end for use in making button loop on one front (this front will be called the left front) and a 5 cm end to secure knitting on other front (the right front).

SLEEVES

Make 2.
Using 4.00 mm needles, cast on 31 (40) stitches.
Work in garter stitch (knit every row), until your knitting measures 6 (8) cm from the cast-on row.
Cast off all 31 (40) stitches, leaving a 5 cm end to secure knitting.

MAKE UP

Using a large blunt needle, sew up shoulder seams for 5 (6) cm and side seams for 4 (6) cm. Sew up side seams of sleeves and sew sleeves in position to back and fronts. Using a 4.00 mm crochet hook and holding length of yarn left at top of the left front, make 6 (8) chain loops (see diagram page 58). Fasten off by cutting off yarn 8 cm from last chain loop and pulling end through last chain loop. Sew this end back into edge 2 cm

below where loops began. To secure, the end should be threaded through to wrong side and darned in for approx 5 cm neatly along edge of knitting. Thread any other loose ends back into seams in same way. Sew on button to corner of right front to match button loop.

Socks

Make 2.
Using 4.00 mm needles, cast on 30 (37) stitches.
Work in garter stitch (knit every row), until your knitting measures 12 (16) cm from cast-on row.
Cut off yarn 10 cm from stitch on needle.
Do not cast off stitches.

TO FINISH SOCKS

Using a large blunt needle, thread another length of yarn (approx 15 cm long) through all stitches on needle, letting stitches drop off needle as you go. Pull ends of yarn tightly to gather up the stitches and tie ends in a knot. Sew up the side seams of

Best Dressed Bear continued

socks to form a tube. Darn in all loose ends. Place socks on teddy bear and fold over tops to fit legs.

Headband

Using 4.00 mm needles, cast on 5 (7) stitches.

Work in garter stitch (knit every row), until your knitting measures 44 (50) cm from the cast-on row.

Cast off all 5 (7) stitches, leaving 5 cm end to secure.

Darn in loose ends.

Tie the headband around the teddy bear's head.

Tea Time

Measurements

Fits 2–3 cup teapot

You will need

8 ply yarn, 50 g balls

½ ball 1st Colour, ½ Ball 2nd Colour, ½ ball 3rd Colour

1 pair 4.00 mm (No 8) knitting needles, a large tapestry needle for sewing seams, cardboard and scissors to make a pompom

A tea-cosy makes a great present for anyone who enjoys a 'cuppa' and the stripey pattern lets you have great fun choosing colours.

TEA FOR TEDDY TOO

Break off yarn.
Using 3rd Colour, knit 8 rows garter stitch.
Repeat these 24 rows until tea-cosy measures about 17 cm, ending with a complete stripe.
Using same colour, cast off.
Darn in ends.
Make another piece the same.

MAKE UP

Using a flat seam, sew up side seams (the cast-on and cast-off edges of your pieces), leaving about 7 cm in the centre of each side for the spout and the handle. Using double yarn, make long running stitches along top edge of tea-cosy, pull up tightly and secure with lots of small stitches along inside of side seam.
Using cardboard 7 cm in diameter with a 1.5 cm centre hole and following instructions on page 20, make a pompom using all 3 colours. Sew securely to the top of the tea-cosy.

Tea-cosy

Using 4.00 mm needles and 1st Colour, cast on 32 stitches.
Knit 8 rows garter stitch. (This means 4 ridges on each side of your work.)
Break off yarn. Always leave enough yarn to darn in end.
Using 2nd Colour, knit 8 rows garter stitch.

WARM UP FOR A WORKOUT

Warm and Woolly

Believe it or not, this jumper, leg warmers

and the headband are all knitted in perfectly plain stitches. All you'll need is a little patience to be able to add some great garments to your winter wardrobe.

Measurements

Jumper

To fit chest:	66–71 cm	76–81 cm
Actual measurement:		
	81	93
Length to back of neck:		
	53	58
Sleeve seam (including 8 cm turn back for cuff):	43	47

Leg warmers

Length (approx):	49	49

Headband

Width (approx):	9	9
Length (approx):	45	45

Note: If you knit the smaller jumper, follow the numbers **outside** the brackets in the pattern; if you knit the larger jumper, follow the numbers **inside** the brackets.

You will need

8 ply yarn, 50 g balls

Jumper: 12 (15) balls Main Colour

Leg warmers: 5 balls Main Colour, 1 ball Contrast Colour

Headband: 1 ball Main Colour

1 pair 4.00 mm (No 8) knitting needles, a large tapestry needle for sewing up seams, 100 cm (approx) hat elastic for leg warmers

Jumper

BACK AND FRONT

Both are knitted the same.
Using 4.00 mm needles and Main Colour cast on 87 (99) stitches.
1st row Knit. (This is the wrong side of your work.)
Repeat 1st row until work measures 53 (58) cm from beginning, working last row on wrong side.
Cast off all stitches. Break off yarn.

SLEEVES

Both are knitted the same.
Using 4.00 mm needles and Main Colour cast on 73 (81) stitches.
1st row Knit. (This is the right side of your work.)
Repeat 1st row until sleeve measures 43 (47) cm from beginning, working last row on wrong side.
Cast off all stitches.
Break off yarn.

MAKE UP

Place back and front together with wrong sides facing out. Sew up the two shoulder seams leaving 23 (25) cm free at centre for neck opening. Sew up side seams, leaving 17 (19) cm

STRETCH IN STYLE

39

free at top edge for armhole. With wrong side facing out sew up sleeve seam, reversing seam for 8 cm at wrist for cuff. With wrong side facing out, matching sleeve seam to side seam, sew the sleeves to the body (pin these in place first to make sewing easier). Turn jumper to right side. Fold back cuff for 8 cm.

1st row Knit.
Repeat this row until colour stripe measures 3 cm working last row on wrong side.
Join in Main Colour.
Next row Knit.
Repeat this row until this stripe measures 3 cm from beginning, working last row on wrong side.
Join in Contrast Colour.
Next row Knit.
Repeat this row until this stripe measures 3 cm working last row on wrong side.
Cast off all stitches.
Break off yarn.

MAKE UP
With wrong sides facing out, sew up leg seam. Thread two rows of elastic through the top edge and one row through the lower edge of each leg warmer on the wrong side. Pull elastic and tighten so leg warmers fit snuggly.

Leg warmers
Both are knitted the same and one size fits both sizes.
Using 4.00 mm knitting needles and Main Colour, cast on 80 stitches.
1st row Knit. (This is wrong side of your work.)
Repeat 1st row until work measures 40 cm from beginning, working last row on wrong side.
Join in Contrast Colour.

Headband
Using 4.00 mm knitting needles and Main Colour, cast on 21 stitches.
1st row Knit. (This is wrong side of your work.)
Repeat 1st row until headband measures 44 (46) cm, (or a length that suits your head), working last row on wrong side.
Cast off all stitches.
Break off yarn.

MAKE UP
Plaee first row and last row together and sew seam.

All Dolled Up

Measurements

Height of doll:	36 cm	41 cm

Jumper

Actual measurement around chest:

	24	26

Length from lower edge to shoulder:

	12	14
Length of sleeve:	7	9

Skirt

Length from waist to lower edge:

	11	13

Cap

To fit head:	30	32

You will need

8 ply yarn, 50 g balls

Jumper, skirt and cap: 2 balls Main Colour, 1 ball Contrast Colour

1 pair 4.00 mm (No 8) knitting needles, a large tapestry needle for sewing seams, 2 Velcro spots for jumper

A cute little jumper, skirt and cap to knit for your favourite doll. The outfit also makes a great present for any younger members of your family.

Jumper

BACK

Using 4.00 mm needles and Contrast Colour, cast on 28 (30) stitches.

1st row Knit. (This is the wrong side.)

Repeat last row 4 times.

Break off Contrast Colour.

Join in Main Colour

Next row Knit.

Next row Purl.

Repeat last 2 rows till work measures 11 (13) cm from cast-on edge.
Break off Main Colour.
Join in Contrast Colour.
Next row Knit.
Repeat last row 3 times more.
Cast off.

FRONT

Knit another piece exactly the same as the back.

SLEEVES

Make 2.
Using 4.00 mm needles and Contrast Colour, cast on 26 (28) stitches.
1st row Knit. (This is the wrong side.)
Repeat last row 4 times more.
Break off Contrast Colour.
Join in Main Colour.
Next row Knit.
Next row Purl.
Repeat last 2 rows till work measures 9 (11) cm from cast-on edge.
Cast off.

MAKE UP

Overlap Front over Back at shoulder and sew together at armhole edge only. Fold sleeves in half and, placing centre of sleeve to shoulder seam, sew in sleeves to back and front. Using backstitch, sew up sides and sleeve seams. Sew a velcro spot at each shoulder, on the right side of the back and the wrong side of the front (which overlaps the back).

Skirt

Make 2 pieces.
Using 4.00 mm needles and Contrast Colour, cast on 44 (48) stitches.
1st row Knit. (This is the wrong side.)
Repeat last row 4 times more.
Break off Contrast Colour.
Join in Main Colour.
6th row Knit.
7th row Purl.
8th row K11 (13), slip the next stitch onto your needle *without* knitting it, K1, pass the slip stitch over the knitted stitch, K18, K2 together, K11 (13).
9th row Purl.
Repeat the last 4 rows 2 (4) times. You should have 38 (38) stitches left on your needle.
Repeat 8th and 9th rows 4 (3) times. You should have 30 (32) stitches left on your needle.
Next row Knit.
Repeat last row 5 times more.
Cast off *very loosely*.

MAKE UP

Using backstitch, sew up side seams. Using finger knitting (see opposite) make a cord 40 cm long and thread it in and out through the middle row of the garter stitch waistband. Tie in a bow at front.

Cap

Using 4.00 mm needles and Main Colour, cast on 58 (66) stitches.
1st row Knit.
2nd row Purl.
Repeat last 2 rows 10 (13) times more. To shape the crown of the cap, you will now decrease as follows:

continued on page 44

FINGER KNITTING

Finger knitting is a quick and simple way to make a chain from wool.

1 Tie a loop of one end of your yarn around your index finger and make a secure knot.

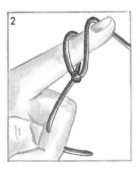

2 Put the longer part of your yarn over your finger in front of this loop. Do not make a knot this time.

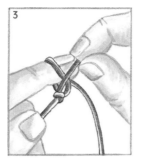

3 Lift the first, back loop up and forward over the front loop and drop it off your finger.

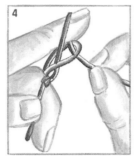

4 This makes your first knitted stitch. Pull your bottom short thread gently down to tighten the stitch.

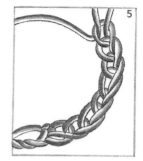

5 Put more wool over in front of the loop you have left on your finger and lift the back loop over and off' again. Repeat this until you have a long enough chain.

Finish off by breaking off your yarn, slipping the loop off your finger, pushing the end of the yarn through the loop and pulling it tight.

1st row K1, * K6, K2 together. Repeat from * to last stitch. You should now have 51 (58) stitches on your needle.

2nd row Purl.

3rd row K1, * K5, K2 together. Repeat from * to last stitch, K1. You should now have 44 (50) stitches on your needle.

4th row Purl.

5th row K1, * K4, K2 together. Repeat from * to last stitch, K1. You should now have 37 (42) stitches on your needle.

6th row Purl.

7th row K1, * K3, K2 together. Repeat from * to last stitch, K1. You should now have 30 (34) stitches on your needle.

8th row Purl.

9th row K1, * K2, K2 together. Repeat from * to last stitch, K1. You should now have 23 (26) stitches on your needle.

10th row Purl.

11th row K1, * K1, K2 together. Repeat from * to last stitch, K1. You should now have 16 (18) stitches on your needle.

12th row Purl.

13th row K1, * K2 together. Repeat from * to last stitch, K1. You should now have 9 (10) stitches on your needle.

14th row Purl.

Break off yarn, leaving a length of thread. Thread end through remaining stitches on needle. Draw up and fasten off securely.

MAKE UP

Using a flat seam, sew up side seam. Roll lower edge up to desired depth of cap.

Out and About

This shoulder bag is just the thing for carrying all those little bits and pieces you need when you're out.

Measurements

Width (approx): 15.5 cm
Depth (approx): 14 cm

You will need

8 ply yarn, 50 g balls

1 ball 1st Colour; ¼ ball 2nd Colour; small quantity 3rd Colour

1 pair 4.00 mm (No 8) knitting needles, a large tapestry needle for sewing seams, 1 large button (optional)

Shoulder bag

Using 4.00 mm needles and 1st Colour, cast on 33 stitches.
Knit 4 rows garter stitch. (This means 2 ridges on each side of your work.)
5th row Knit.
6th row Purl.
Repeating 5th and 6th rows will produce stocking stitch. Work in stocking stitch until work measures 26 cm from beginning, ending with a purl row.
Break off yarn. Always leave enough yarn to darn in the end.

BEGIN FRONT FLAP

Using 2nd Colour, knit 14 rows garter stitch. (This means 7 ridges on each side of your work.)
Using 3rd Colour, knit 4 rows garter stitch (2 ridges on each side).
Using 2nd Colour, knit 12 rows garter stitch (6 ridges on each side).
Cast off.

MAKE UP

Fold bag so that the cast-on edge is level with the first row of the front flap (the smooth side of the stocking stitch goes on the outside). Using a flat seam sew up the side seams. If

you wish, make a tassel from the 3rd Colour to use as a fastening, or you can use a button. Stitch a loop in the centre of the front flap large enough for the button or tassel. Sew the button or tassel underneath and fold flap over.

TO MAKE THE STRAP

Cut 4 pieces of each colour 114 cm long and plait together, tying a knot at each end.

Stitch neatly to each side of the top of the bag so that the knots of the plaits are under the front flap.

Happy Harry

'Clothes maketh the man.' This is especially true of Harry whose clothes, except for his jacket, are part of him.

Measurements
Height (approx): 22 cm

You will need
8 ply yarn, 50 g balls

½ ball fawn, ½ ball purple, ½ ball red, small quantity light green, small quantity teal, small quantity medium green

1 pair 3.25 mm (No 10) knitting needles, a large tapestry needle for sewing seams, some washable filling

Doll

BODY AND HEAD

Using 3.25 mm needles and purple, cast on 40 stitches.

Knit 20 rows garter stitch — knit every row. (This means 10 ridges on each side of your work.)

Break off yarn. (Always leave enough yarn to darn in end.)

Join in light green.

Next row Knit.

Do not break off light green but join in teal.

Next row Purl.

Do not break off teal but join in medium green.

Next row Knit.

Continue working in stocking stitch (1 row knit, 1 row purl) in one row each of these 3 colours until you have 14 stripes altogether.

Break off all 3 colours and join in fawn. Work 26 rows in stocking stitch.

Next row K2 (this means to knit 2 stitches), * K2 together (see page 12), K1. Repeat the section beginning from * until the end of the row. You should have 28 stitches left on your needle.

Next row Purl.
Next row * K2 together. Repeat from * until the end of the row. You should have 14 stitches left.
Break off yarn, leaving an end about 25 cm long.
Thread a large tapestry needle with the long end and thread this through the stitches remaining on the needle, slipping the stitches off the needle as you go. Pull up the end tightly (so the top of the head is gathered) and fasten securely with small stitches. Using backstitch and the same thread, sew up the centre back seam of the head. Continue sewing up the centre back seam using one of the stripe colours for the shirt and purple for the trousers. Fill the head and body, leaving a slightly less well filled section at the neck. Using a flat seam, sew up lower edge of trousers. Using a double length of fawn, secure end at centre back at end of stripes. Gather neck by making a row of running stitches around the first row of fawn and pulling up tightly. Fasten off securely with lots of small stitches.
Embroider face as shown in the photograph. To make hair, thread needle with a double length of red yarn. Beginning at side of face, make a couple of small stitches to secure end. Make another small stitch in the same place, leaving a loop the size of 2 fingers, then make another small stitch to secure. Repeat these 2 stitches in rows across head until hair looks thick enough.

LEGS
Make 2 the same.
Using 3.25 mm needles and red, cast on 21 stitches.
Knit 14 rows garter stitch. (This means 7 ridges on each side of your work.)
Break off red and join in medium green.
** **Next row** Knit.
Do not break off medium green but join in teal.
Next row Purl.
Do not break off teal but join in light green.
Next row Knit **.
Continue working in stocking stitch in one row each of these 3 colours until you have 12 stripes altogether.
Break off all 3 colours and join in fawn.
Work 12 rows stocking stitch.
Break off fawn and join in purple.
Knit 10 rows garter stitch.
Cast off.
Fold leg in half lengthways and using a flat seam, sew up lower edge of foot. Using backstitch and matching colours (as before) sew up side of leg. Fill leg then using a flat seam, sew upper edge together. Using red, gather above foot (as at the neck). Tie a length of purple around the ankle and finish with a bow. Sew legs to lower edge of body.

ARMS
Make 2 the same.
Using 3.25 mm needles and fawn, cast on 16 stitches.
Knit 10 rows garter stitch. (This means 5 ridges on each side of your work.)
Work 8 rows stocking stitch.
Break off fawn and join in medium green.
Work as for Leg from ** to **.

Continued on page 49

Bag a Bottle

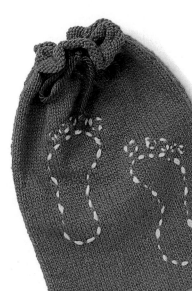

Anyone who takes a 'hotty' to bed will love this very practical hot water bottle bag. Every night when they put their cold feet on it, they'll think of you.

Measurements
To fit a standard hot water bottle — approx 28 cm x 21 cm

You will need
8 ply yarn, 50 g balls
2 balls

1 pair 4.00 mm (No 8) knitting needles, a large tapestry needle for sewing seams, 60 cm cord or ribbon for threading through top of bag

Hot water bottle bag

Using 4.00 mm needles, cast on 50 stitches.

1st row Knit. (This is the right side.)

2nd row Purl. (This is the wrong side.)

Repeating 1st and 2nd rows will produce stocking stitch. Repeat 1st and 2nd rows until your knitting measures 64 cm from the cast-on edge, finishing with a purl row.

Cast off all stitches leaving a 5 cm end to sew into seam when finishing.

FEET EMBROIDERY
With a pencil draw around your feet (or hands) on a piece of paper. Cut out the shapes and pin them onto your bag. Using a double thread of a contrasting colour, stitch around the shapes using a simple tacking stitch. Remove the paper shapes.

MAKE UP
Fold fabric in half (the centre row of the bag is the fold line) so that

the right sides are together (the wrong sides should be on the outside). Using a large blunt needle, sew the two side edges together, leaving the cast-on and cast-off edges free. Darn in all loose ends and turn the bag right side out. The cast-on and cast-off edges will roll onto the right side for a few rows by themselves and this will give you a nice edge at the top. Begin in the centre of one side of your bag, about 3 cm down from the top edge, and thread the ribbon in and out of your knitting in a straight line around the top of the bag. Draw ends up firmly and tie in a bow.

Happy Harry continued

Continue working in stocking stitch until you have 10 stripes altogether.
Cast off.
Fold arm in half lengthways and using a flat seam, sew up lower edge of hand. Using backstitch and matching colours (as before) sew up side of arm. Fill arm but do not sew end together. Using fawn, gather above garter stitch (as at neck) to form hand. Place against body so that end of arm is a circle and using colour of cast-off row, sew arm to body.

Jacket

Using 3.25 mm needles and purple, cast on 43 stitches.
Knit 4 rows garter stitch. (This means 2 ridges on each side.)

DIVIDE FOR FRONTS AND BACK

Next row K5, cast off 4 stitches,

K25 (this includes the stitch left on your right-hand needle after casting off at the underarm), cast off 4 stitches, K5.
Continue on last 5 sts for left front.
Knit 13 rows garter stitch (9 ridges on each side of your work altogether from the cast-on).
Cast off.
Join yarn to next group of 25 stitches for the back.
Knit 13 rows garter stitch.
Cast off.
Join yarn to last group of 5 stitches for right front.
Knit 13 rows garter stitch.
Cast off.
Using a flat seam, sew fronts to top of back to form shoulders, leaving the centre 15 cast-off stitches to form the back neck.

Bow tie

Using 3.25 mm needles and red, cast on 5 stitches.
Knit in garter stitch until bow tie measures 24 cm.
Cast off.
Darn in ends and tie around neck in a knot.

Picnic Partners

With clever use of colour, you can make something that is incredibly easy to knit look really special. For a really big rug, why not get your friends to help you knit some of the squares.

Measurements

1 square is approx 13 cm x 13 cm
Rug: 12 squares x 12 squares
Cushion: 3 squares x 3 squares

You will need

12 ply wool, 50 g balls

Rug: 8 balls blue (includes enough for fringe), 7 balls red, 7 balls green, 7 balls yellow

Cushion: 3 balls blue (includes enough for fringe), 2 balls red, 2 balls green, 2 balls yellow

1 pair 5.50 mm (No 5) knitting needles, a large tapestry needle for sewing seams, a large crochet hook for making tassels on rug, polyester fibre for cushion

Rug

81 squares.

FIRST SQUARE

Using 5.50 mm needles and blue yarn, cast on 21 stitches.
1st row Knit.
Work in garter stitch (knit every row), until your knitting measures 13 cm from the cast-on row.
Cast off all 21 stitches, leaving a 5 cm end to sew into seam when squares have been sewn together.
Make a total of 21 blue squares, 20 red squares, 20 green squares and 20 yellow squares.

MAKE UP

Sew the squares together in the order shown on the diagram (see page 52), using large blunt needle. It may be easier to sew 9 strips of 9 squares together first and then join all these strips together. Darn in loose ends along seams, using large blunt needle.

Note: *Instead of working 81 squares for the rug, you may wish to knit 9 strips that are 9 squares long. Follow the instructions for the squares but instead of casting off keep knitting in blocks of colours as shown on the diagram (change colours only when you have worked an odd number of rows). Sew the strips together in the order shown on the diagram and darn in all loose ends, using large blunt needle.*

FRINGE

Cut 7 lengths of blue yarn 20 cm long. Holding all 7 lengths and using a crochet hook, insert hook through edge of rug from right side to wrong side and draw centre of lengths through fabric to form a loop on right side. Draw ends of lengths through loop firmly to form a tassel (see diagrams 1, 2 and 3 on page 18). Work tassels in blue evenly around all edges of rug.

Cushion

18 squares.
Make 5 blue squares, 5 red squares, 4 green squares and 4 yellow squares.

MAKE UP

Sew the squares together in the order shown on the diagram (see page 52), using large blunt needle. It may be easier to sew 3 strips of 3 squares together first and then join all these strips together. You should now have 2 pieces 3 squares wide and

3 squares long. Place right sides of pieces together and sew pieces together, leaving an opening one square wide on one side. Darn in any

Picnic Partners continued

loose ends along seams, using large blunt needle. Turn the cushion inside out. Fill cushion and sew up opening.

Note: *Instead of working 18 squares for the cushion, you may wish to knit 6 strips that are 3 squares long. Follow the instructions for the squares but instead of casting off keep knitting in blocks of colour as shown on the diagram (change colours only when you have worked an odd number of rows). Sew the strips together in the order shown on the diagram and darn in all loose ends, using a large blunt needle.*

Target Practice

GUIDE FOR SEWING UP
CUSHION PIECES

R	Y	G
B	R	Y
G	B	R

First piece

B	R	Y
G	B	R
Y	G	B

Second piece

GUIDE FOR SEWING UP RUG

B	R	Y	G	B	R	Y	G	B
R	Y	G	B	R	Y	G	B	R
Y	G	B	R	Y	G	B	R	Y
G	B	R	Y	G	B	R	Y	G
B	R	Y	G	B	R	Y	G	B
R	Y	G	B	R	Y	G	B	R
Y	G	B	R	Y	G	B	R	Y
G	B	R	Y	G	B	R	Y	G
B	R	Y	G	B	R	Y	G	B

A great addition to any bedroom, this comfy cushion is very easy to knit. Try not to choose a combination of colours that will make your parents groan!

Measurements

30 cm x 30 cm

You will need

12 ply yarn, 50 g balls
1 ball Main Colour
1 ball Contrast Colour

1 pair 5.00 mm (No 6) knitting needles, a large tapestry needle for sewing seams, wadding for filling or a small pillow

Cushion

CENTRE PIECES

Make 2.
Using 5.00 mm needles and Main Colour, cast on 32 stitches.
1st row Knit.
2nd row Purl.
Repeat last 2 rows until work measures 20 cm from cast-on edge.
Cast off.

SHORT OUTSIDE PIECE

Make 2.
Using 5.00 mm needles and Contrast Colour, cast on 9 stitches.
1st row Knit. (This is the wrong side.)
Repeat last row until work measures 20 cm from cast-on edge.
Cast off.

LONG OUTSIDE PIECE

Make 2.
Using 5.00 mm needles and Contrast Colour, cast on 9 stitches.
1st row Knit. (This is the wrong side.)
Repeat last row until work measures 30 cm from cast-on edge.
Cast off.

MAKE UP

Place wrong sides of centre pieces together, and sew 3 sides together. Using a flat seam, sew one short outside piece to edge opposite opening and the other short piece to one edge of centre piece opening. Sew the long pieces along top edges of short pieces and side of centre pieces. Fill cushion with wadding or small pillow, then sew up opening.

Writer's Stripes

Measurements
Width (approx): 23 cm
Depth (approx): 14 cm

Impress your school friends with a very different pencil case. Velcro dots make fastening the top easy and you can decorate it with beads as we have or let your imagination run riot.

You will need

8 ply yarn, 50 g balls
1 ball 1st Colour
¼ ball 2nd Colour

1 pair 4.00 mm (No 8) knitting needles, a large tapestry needle for sewing seams, 4 Velcro dots, 12 beads

Pencil Case

Using 4.00 mm needles and 1st Colour, cast on 52 stitches.
Knit 8 rows garter stitch. (This means 4 ridges on each side of your work.)
9th row Knit.
10th row Purl.
Repeating 9th and 10th rows will produce stocking stitch. Repeat 9th and 10th rows 4 times (10 rows altogether).
Do not break off 1st Colour but join in 2nd Colour.

Using 2nd Colour, work 2 rows stocking stitch.

Before knitting the next row, wind the 2nd Colour once around the 1st Colour so that the 1st Colour can be carried neatly at the side of your work.

Work 2 rows stocking stitch, then wind colours as before.

Work 2 rows stocking stitch.

Do not break off 2nd Colour but pick up 1st Colour again. (Take care not to pull it too tightly or the side of your work will gather up.)

Work 6 rows stocking stitch, winding colours as before after each purl row.

Change to 2nd Colour and work 4 rows stocking stitch, winding colours as before.

Change to 1st Colour and work 4 rows stocking stitch, winding colours as before.

Change to 2nd Colour and work 2 rows stocking stitch.

Break off 2nd Colour. Always leave end long enough to darn in.

Using 1st Colour, work 44 rows stocking stitch, then knit 8 rows garter stitch.

Cast off.

MAKE UP

Fold pencil case in half and using a flat seam, sew up side seams. Cut 6 lengths of 1st Colour about 15 cm long and thread a bead on each end of each length (see diagram). Tie a large knot close to each end to stop the beads falling off. Take 3 lengths with beads and tie them together in the middle with a 20-cm length of yarn. Then fold them in half to form a tassel and wrap one end of the yarn tightly around the fold clockwise and the other end anticlockwise and knot the two ends to secure them. Sew the tassel to one end of the pencil case opening. Repeat at the other end. Glue Velcro dots to each side of opening.

MAKING A TASSEL FOR THE PENCIL CASE

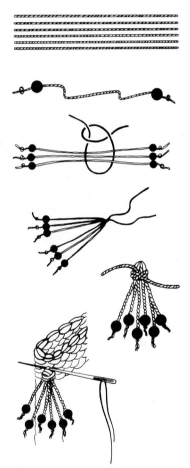

55

Tiny Tots

Measurements
Height (approx): 26 cm

You will need
8 ply yarn, 50 g balls
½ ball 1st Colour (C1), ½ ball 2nd Colour (C2), ½ ball 3rd Colour (C3), ½ ball 4th Colour (C4), ½ ball 5th Colour (C5)

1 pair 3.75 mm (No 9) knitting needles, a 2.5 mm crochet hook, a large safety pin, pink and blue embroidery cotton or scraps of wool, a large tapestry needle for sewing seams, washable soft toy filling

These cute little twins can be seen and not heard, so they can't cause too much trouble and it will be quite safe to add them to your family.

Doll with bib

LEGS
These are worked from the top downwards.
Make 2.
Using 3.75 mm needles and C1 cast on 18 stitches.

Knit 16 rows in garter stitch.

Break off yarn.

Using C2 knit 4 rows garter stitch.

Next row * K2, K2 together.*
Repeat from * to * till last 2 stitches,
K2. You should have 14 stitches left.

Knit 3 rows garter stitch.

Next row * K1, K2 together.*
Repeat from * to * to last 2 stitches,
K2. You should have 10 stitches left.

Break off yarn leaving an end long
enough for sewing.

Thread a piece of cotton through a
tapestry needle and thread this cotton through the stitches remaining
on the needle, slipping the stitches
off the needle as you go. Pull the
cotton tight (so the end of the leg
is gathered) and knot the ends
together.

ARMS

*These are worked from the top
downwards.*
Make 2.

Using 3.75 mm needles and C1 cast
on 16 stitches.

Knit 12 rows garter stitch.

Break off yarn.

Using C3 knit 4 rows garter stitch.

Next row * K2, K2 together.*
Repeat from * to * to end of row.
You should have 12 stitches left.

Knit 3 rows garter stitch.

Next row * K1, K2 together.*
Repeat from * to * to end of row.
Break off yarn leaving an end long
enough for sewing.

Thread a piece of cotton through a
tapestry needle and thread this cotton through the stitches remaining
on the needle, slipping the stitches
off the needle as you go. Pull the
cotton tight (so the end of the arm
is gathered) and knot the ends
together.

BODY AND HEAD

This is worked from the bottom up.
Make 1.

Using 3.75 mm needles and C1 cast
on 40 stitches.

Knit 37 rows garter stitch.

Next row K8, K2 together twice, K6,
K2 together twice, K8. You should
have 36 stitches left.

Next row K5, cast off 8 stitches,
K10, cast off 8 stitches, K5. You should
have 20 stitches left.

(The cast-off stitches form the
shoulders. Leave these unworked.)

Next row K5, K10 stitches (front of
doll), K5.

Knit 2 rows garter stitch.

Break off yarn.

Change to C3 to begin the head.

**1st row Knit.

2nd row Purl.

3rd row Increase in each stitch (see
page 11). You should have 40 stitches
on your needle.

4th row Purl.

5th row K10, increase in next stitch,
K18, increase in next stitch, K10. You
should have 42 stitches on your
needle.

6th row Purl.

7th row Knit.

8th row Purl.

9th row K11, increase in next stitch,
K18, increase in next stitch, K11. You
should have 44 stitches on your
needle.

10th row Purl.

11th row Knit.

12th row Purl.

13th row Knit.

14th row Purl.

15th row K10, K2 together, K20, K2 together, K10. You should have 42 stitches left.
16th row Purl.
17th row Knit.
18th row Purl.
19th row K10, K2 together, K18, K2 together, K10. You should have 40 stitches left.
20th row Purl.
21st row *K1, K2 together.* Repeat from * to * to last stitch, K1. You should have 27 stitches left.
22nd row Purl.
23rd row Knit.
24th row Purl.
25th row K2 together to last stitch, K1. You should have 14 stitches left. Break off yarn leaving end long enough for sewing.
Thread a piece of cotton through a tapestry needle and thread this cotton through the stitches remaining on the needle, slipping the stitches off the needle as you go. Pull the cotton tight and knot the ends together.

BIB

This is worked from the bottom up. Make 1.
Using 3.75 mm needles and C4, cast on 15 stitches.
Knit 4 rows garter stitch.
5th row Knit.
6th row K2, P11 (this means purl 11 stitches — bring the wool from the back of your knitting to the front when changing from a knit stitch to a purl stitch, and when you have finished the purl stitches, take the wool to the back again), K2.
Repeat 5th and 6th rows 9 times.
Next row K4, cast off 7 stitches, K4.

Put the stitches on the left-hand side on a safety pin and continue on the right-hand side.
Next row K2, P2.
Next row Knit.
Repeat last 2 rows twice.
Next row Cast off 2 stitches.
Pull the knitting needle out of the 2 remaining stitches. Using a crochet needle, hook one loop through the other, and crochet 30 chains for the tie (see illustration). Fasten off.
Left side
Put the 4 stitches on the left side back onto the knitting needle.
Next row K2, P2.
Next row Knit.
Repeat last 2 rows twice.
Cast off 2 stitches.
Pull the knitting needle out of the 2 remaining stitches. Using a crochet needle, hook one loop through the other, and crochet 30 chains for the tie. Fasten off.

MAKE UP

Using 6 strands of pink embroidery cotton, embroider the mouth with 3 satin stitches over the centre stitch of the 8th row of the head. Using

CROCHET CHAIN FOR TINY TOT'S BIB

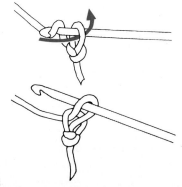

light blue embroidery cotton, work the eyes with 2 satin stitches in the 12th row 7 stitches apart. Cut about 36 pieces of yellow wool, each about 4 cm long. Knot these onto the top of the head from the 21st row. Use the crochet hook to pull each piece of wool through one knitted stitch. When it is pulled halfway through, tie the two ends together in a double knot. Tie a bow made of contrasting wool into the hair.

Fold the wrong sides of the body and head piece together and using a flat seam sew the back seam of the body and head together. Sew the shoulders together. Fill the body firmly with the washable filling, using small pieces of filling at a time and taking care not to push the knitting out of shape. Sew the lower edge of the body.

Work a row of running stitches through the neck; that is, the first row of the head. Pull the thread gently and tie the ends together. Tuck the ends inside the doll. Sew the back seams of the legs and the back seams of the arms. Fill the arms and legs and sew the top edges together. Sew the arms and legs to the body.

Striped doll

LEGS

These are worked from the top downwards.
Make 2.
Using 3.75 mm needles and C5 cast on 18 stitches.
Knit 16 rows garter stitch.
Break off yarn.

Using C2 knit 4 rows garter stitch. Repeat as for legs in doll with bib from ** to end.

LITTLE PALS FOR LITTLE GALS

Tiny Tots continued

ARMS

These are worked from the top downwards.
Make 2.
Using 3.75 mm needles and C1 cast on 16 stitches.
Knit 2 rows garter stitch.
Using C5 knit 2 rows garter stitch.
Repeat last 4 rows twice.
Break off yarn.
Using C3 knit 4 rows garter stitch.
Repeat as for arms in doll with bib from ** to end.

BODY AND HEAD

This is worked from the bottom up.
Make 1.
Using 3.75 mm needles and C5 cast on 40 stitches.
Knit 12 rows in garter stitch.
Using C1 knit 2 rows in garter stitch.
Using C5 knit 2 rows in garter stitch.
Repeat last 4 rows 5 times.
Using C1 knit 1 row garter stitch.
Next row Knit 8, knit 2 together twice, knit 16, knit 2 together twice, knit 8. You should have 36 stitches left on your needle.
Next row Using C5, knit 5, cast off 8 stitches, knit 10, cast off 8 stitches, knit 5. You should have 20 stitches left on your needle.
(The cast-off stitches form the shoulders. Leave these unworked.)
Next row Knit 5, knit 10 stitches (front of doll), knit 5 stitches.
Using C1 knit 2 rows garter stitch.
Break off yarn.
Change to C3 to begin the head.
Repeat as for body and head in doll with bib from ** to end.

MAKE UP

Make up as for doll with bib.

Brilliant Baggage

They'll see you coming with this patchwork tote bag. You can follow our pattern, or let your imagination run riot and design your own squares.

Measurements

Approx. 35 x 25 cm

You will need

8 ply wool, 50 g balls

2 balls 1st Colour (C1), 2 balls 2nd Colour (C2), 2 balls 3rd Colour (C3), 2 balls 4th Colour (C4)

1 pair 4.00 mm (No 8) knitting needles, 40 cm of 90 cm wide material for lining the bag, 2 m of 2 cm wide grosgrain ribbon, 1 large tapestry needle for sewing dots and seams, 1 large safety pin

KNITTING THE SQUARES

Square 1

Using 4.00 mm needles and C3 cast on 24 stitches.
1st row Knit.
2nd row Purl.
Repeat 1st and 2nd rows 14 times.
Cast off.
Using a tapestry needle and C2 embroider spots randomly in satin stitch. Each spot is two satin stitch bars.

Square 2

Using 4.00 mm needles and C2, cast on 24 stitches.
Knit 44 rows garter stitch.
Cast off.

Square 3

Work as for Square 1 knitting in C1 and using C4 for spots.

Square 4

Work as for Square 2 using C1.

Square 5

Work as for Square 1 knitting in C4 and using C1 for spots.

Square 6

Using 4.00 mm needles and C3, cast on 24 stitches.
Knit 12 rows garter stitch.
Using C2 knit 4 rows garter stitch.
Using C3 knit 12 rows garter stitch.
Using C2 knit 4 rows garter stitch.
Using C3 knit 12 rows garter stitch.
Cast off.

Square 7

Work as for Square 2 using C2.

Square 8

Using 4.00 mm needles and C2 cast on 24 stitches.
Knit 4 rows garter stitch.
Using C4 knit 4 rows garter stitch.
Repeat last 8 rows 4 times.
Using C2 knit 4 rows garter stitch.
Cast off.

Square 9

Work as for Square 2 using C2.
Make a total of 18 squares. You could make another 9 the same as the ones above, or design your own.

BANDS

Make 2.
Using C1 cast on 66 stitches.
1st row Knit.
2nd row Purl.
Repeat 1st and 2nd rows 9 times (so you have 20 rows of stocking stitch in total).
Cast off.

MAKE UP

With a slightly damp cloth and warm iron, press stocking stitch squares and bands. Using a flat seam and a tapestry needle, sew the squares together — 9 for the front and 9 for the back of the bag. Sew 3 squares together to make one strip and then join the strips together.

Placing right sides together, sew a band to the top of each of the sides of the bag, using a flat seam. Fold the band over to the wrong side and sew the band to the top of the knitting. Leave the ends open for the ribbon to be threaded through.

MIX AND MATCH WITH THE PERFECT PATCH

GUIDE FOR SEWING UP BAG PIECES

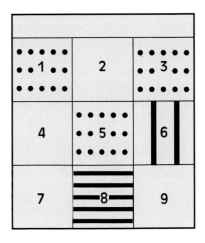

HOW TO MAKE THE LINING
For the lining cut a piece of fabric 70 x 30 cm. Fold in half, right sides together, and sew 1 cm wide side seams.

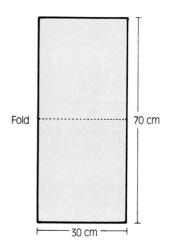

Fold

70 cm

30 cm

SEWING THE LINING

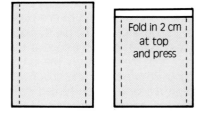

Fold in 2 cm at top and press

At the top of the lining, fold 2 cm of fabric to the wrong side, all round. Press.

FITTING THE LINING

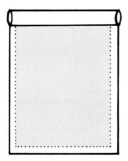

Slip the lining inside the knitted bag, wrong sides together. Line up the top of the lining with the bottom of the top band and hem it in place.

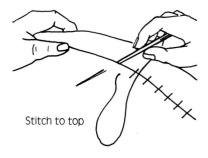

Stitch to top

FINISHING OFF

Cut the ribbon in half. Attach a large safety pin to one end of one piece of ribbon, and use the pin to guide the ribbon through one band at the top and then through the other band. Both ends of the ribbon will be at the same side of the bag. Knot the ends together. Now thread the other piece of ribbon through both bands in the opposite direction. When the two ends are at the opposite side to the first ribbon, knot them together. Pull the ties up and see if they are the right length for you. If they are too long, tie a new knot and cut the ends off.

THREADING THE RIBBONS

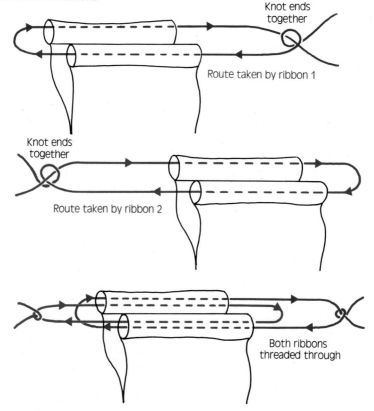

Knot ends together

Route taken by ribbon 1

Knot ends together

Route taken by ribbon 2

Both ribbons threaded through